R35244

D1612678

GIANNI VERSACE

# The Art of Being You

ABBEVILLE PRESS PUBLISHERS
New York  London  Paris

391.092
VER

texts by

**Germano Celant**
**Ingrid Sischy**
**Richard Martin**
**Frank Moore**
**Julian Schnabel**

This book
is a tribute to
a great artist
himself,
to someone
who lived
with
an incredible
love for art,
to a very
special person
who was
always
fascinated
by art and
artists
and always
supported
them,
our brother
**Gianni**

**Donatella
and Santo**

# Thursday/January 22/1987 Milan

Lunch with Gianni Versace, went to his castle. Rizzoli's old castle. Big Roman and Greek statues that Susie Frankfurt got Versace to buy.

# It was grand, huge, so glamorous.

We had a good time. Then had to go back to the gallery to do another press conference at 4:30. Stayed till 8:30 with Daniela coughing in my face and me signing autographs. Gianni did the costumes for Bob Wilson's Salome at La Scala. He got us tickets so I could slip away from my opening when I got tired.

ANDY WARHOL's diary

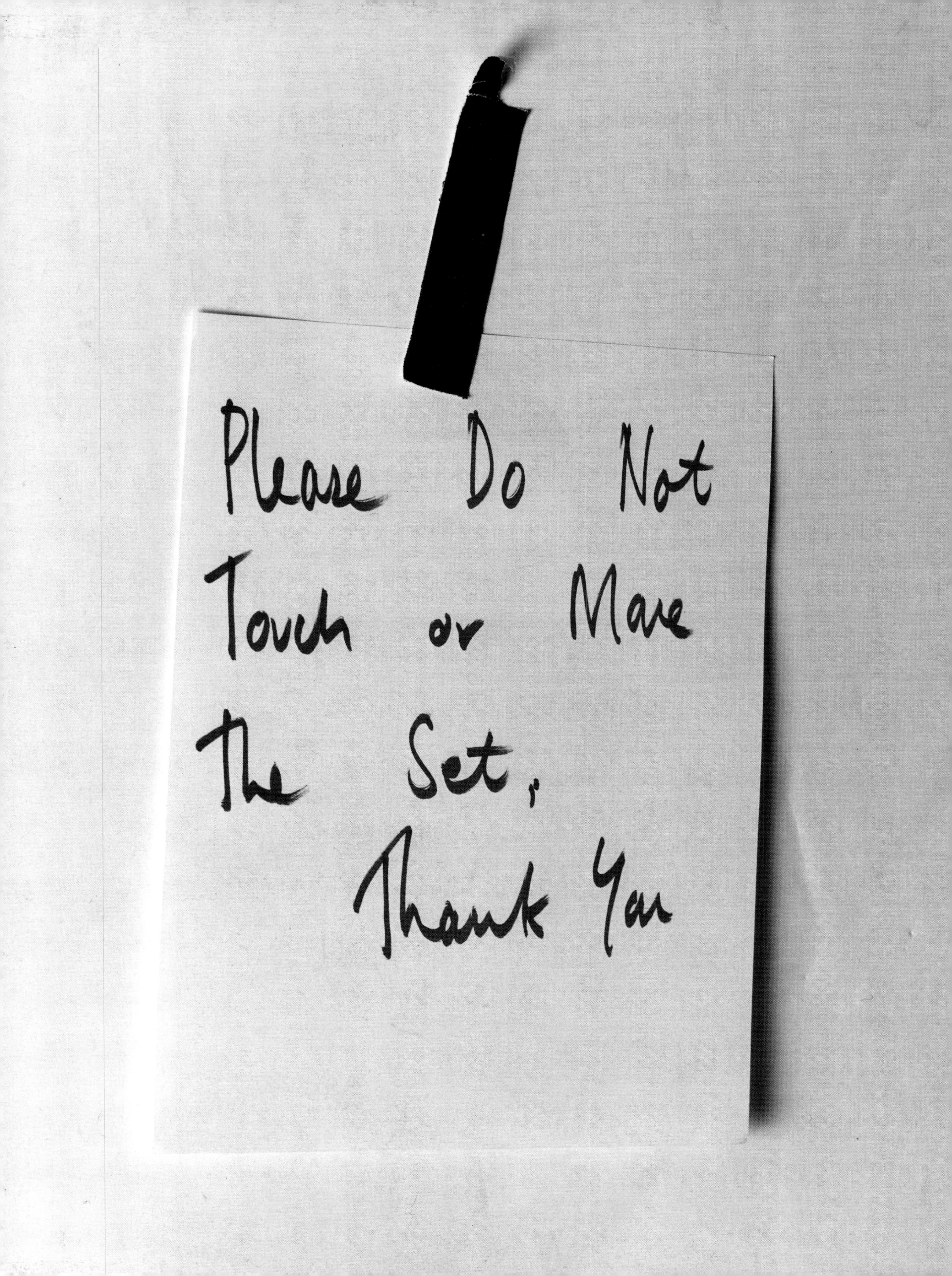
Please Do Not
Touch or Move
The Set,
Thank You

The following text was written in the summer of 1996, a year before Gianni Versace's life was taken, and so cruelly cut short. He was at an ideal point in his life—that point when so much has been achieved and there is still so much to do. The project for which I wrote the following text, *The Art of Being You*, was a boundary-breaking publication, one in which many forms of creativity came together and which Gianni Versace himself initiated and inspired. He had asked *Interview* magazine to work with him and his team on producing a completely new kind of advertising vehicle, a special supplement which could ultimately be an artful gift to readers. In it, his work in fashion, photography from the Versace archives, a variety of art, and statements by Versace all came together to suggest a new way of looking at things. This goal was typical of his character and of his vision. In everything done in the name of the House of Versace, he always wanted it to be driven by a sense of the new—and he always believed that the best engine to take us into the future is creativity. This perspective is so much a part of the Versace way of doing things that it seems almost genetic, and one continues to witness it in action today with the work that's being done at the house. With *The Art of Being You*, I got to see first-hand what it was like to work with Gianni Versace. One experienced an incredible combination of being trusted and being pushed. His high expectations, his belief that nothing was impossible, and his fearlessness were all so convincing and inspiring that it made you feel all those things too. With *The Art of Being You*—which involved commissioning special artwork—Versace's affinities to Andy Warhol, an artist he'd always admired, became ever so clear. Warhol's philosophy, and his ability to see creativity holistically was, like Versace's, ahead of its time. For our supplement, we asked Versace to tell us some of the things that best expressed his philosophy about style, and about life. The first thing he said was, "On each person's shoulders is the freedom to have his or her own style." Versace's life and his work are a testimony to the beauty of that statement. Ingrid Sischy, November 1997

This gift to you from fashion designer Gianni Versace is a celebration of creativity, individualism, and freedom. The individual who sends it to you is someone who exemplifies the art of being himself, and who doesn't waste his energy being afraid of the judgment of others. He says what he thinks, does what he thinks, designs what he thinks. Over and over, when he has spoken about his own field, he has declared that he hates boredom, that he believes people want excitement, glamour, dreams—just as he does. No doubt Versace's perspective comes from his own life. As a kid, he got some great basic lessons in the art of transformation through fashion. He would sit by and watch his mother sewing dresses for her customers. He witnessed the way that materials can alchemize into forms that allow people to feel as if they're stepping into their dreams. Versace's dream of being able to provide this alchemy on a big scale has come true. He's what in America we call "a success story." It makes sense that he'd be such good friends with another success story, a man who, like Versace, is intensely tuned in to human yearning—musician Elton John. He too epitomizes the art of being yourself. There's a beautiful, democratic saying that was invented by Elton John, which Versace loves because it sums up his philosophy: "Some people are born royal. Other people realize their own royalty." I cannot imagine a better way to express the fact that each person has within himself or herself their own richness, their own power, their own glamour, their own kingdom of ideas about what rules in life. This understanding of what is possible in contemporary life is also what made *Interview*'s founder, Andy Warhol, tick. It's what made Warhol want to fill a room (and *Interview* magazine) with a mix of people that included countesses and club kids, icons and individuals who had nowhere to go but with their dreams, to prove the point that one minute somebody could be struggling to get an audition and the next minute become the star that magazines want on their covers. It's telling that when Warhol would run into Gianni Versace (whom he painted), the artist would ask to be in one of the designer's campaigns. If you think about this one way, it's a classic funny anecdote about Warhol's foray into modeling. Let's face it—he wasn't Naomi Campbell. But if you think about Warhol's interest in Versace's pictures in a deeper way, it says a lot about Versace's connection to images. Warhol intuited that in a Versace picture the aura of Warhol's being would come through. Being in a Versace ad also suited Warhol's love of mixing up art and commerce, and of showing how artful commerce could be. I think Warhol would have liked the fact that his work is present in this gift to you from Versace. [ ... ] Fun is not only something that Versace encourages, he honors it. He believes in its medicinal powers—just like he believes in the power of creativity. You can see this belief in action in the photographs that have been done by various photographers for Versace's campaigns over the years; this supplement contains a selection of these images. They are a testimony to the fact that art and commerce can co-exist, and result in work that belongs on a museum wall. Versace wanted you to experience, with this supplement, the same turned-on feeling one can have at a wonderful art show. In fact, in addition to the photographs, you'll notice that, from cover to cover, all the way through, there's lot of wonderful art, most of it created especially for this supplement. So enjoy it all. And have fun reading Versace's how-to philosophy on the art of being you. **Ingrid Sischy**, October 1996

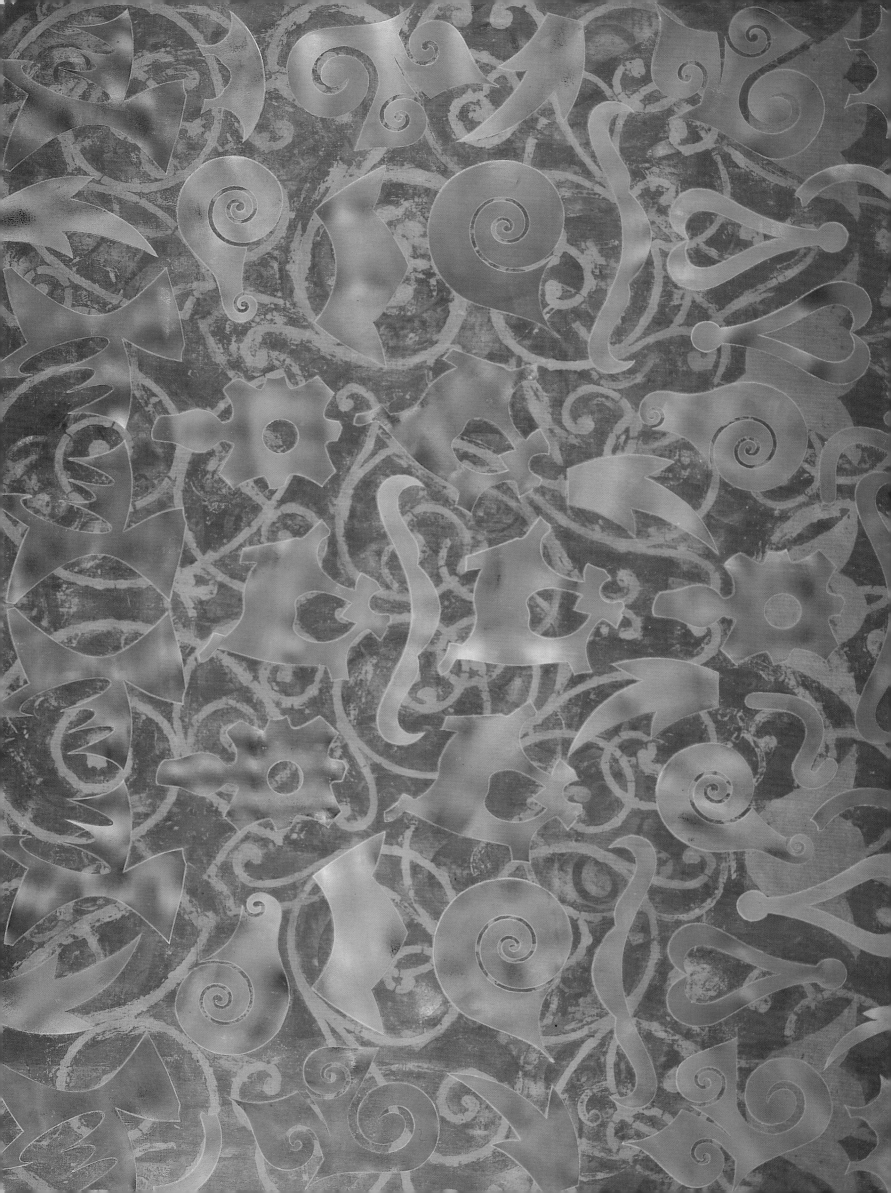

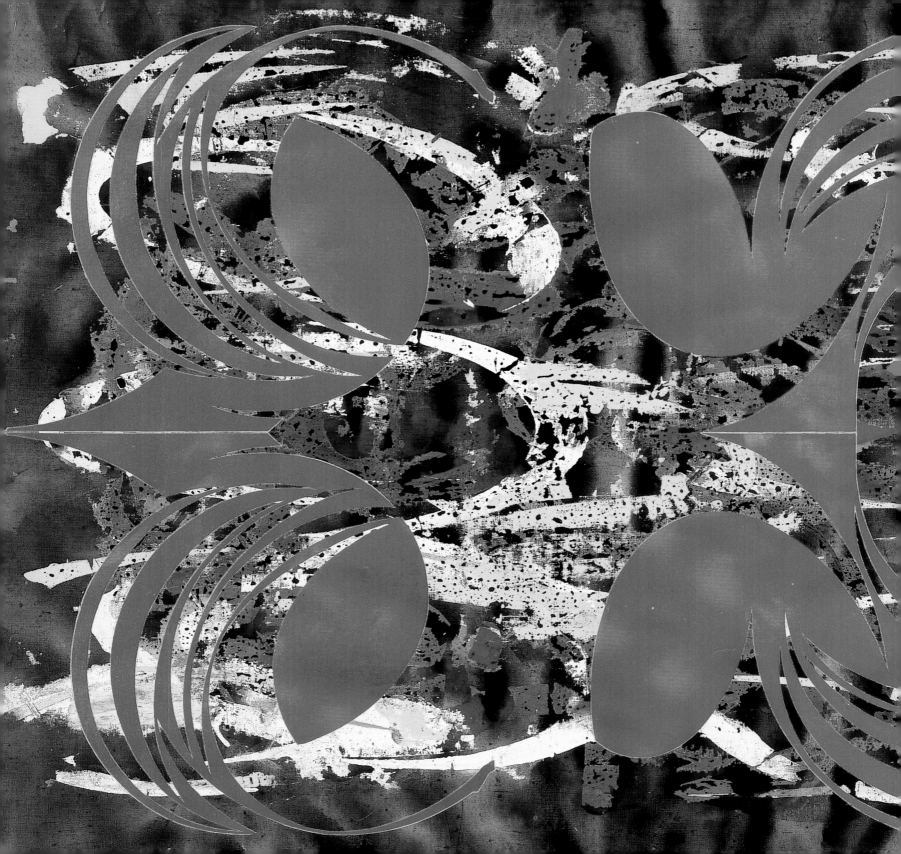

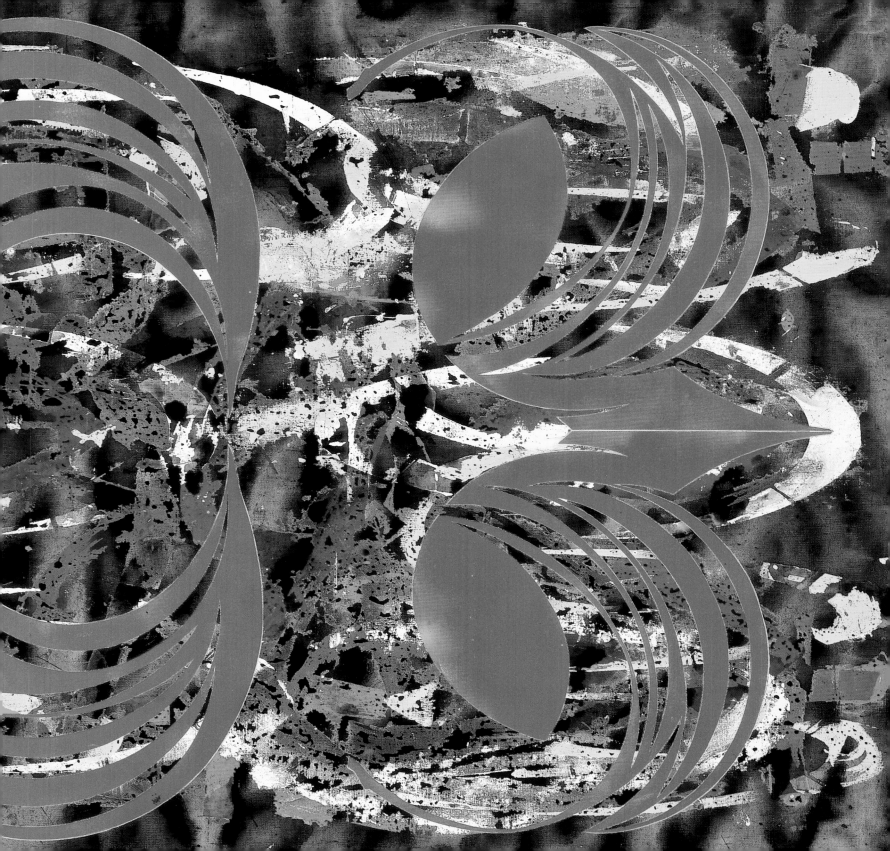

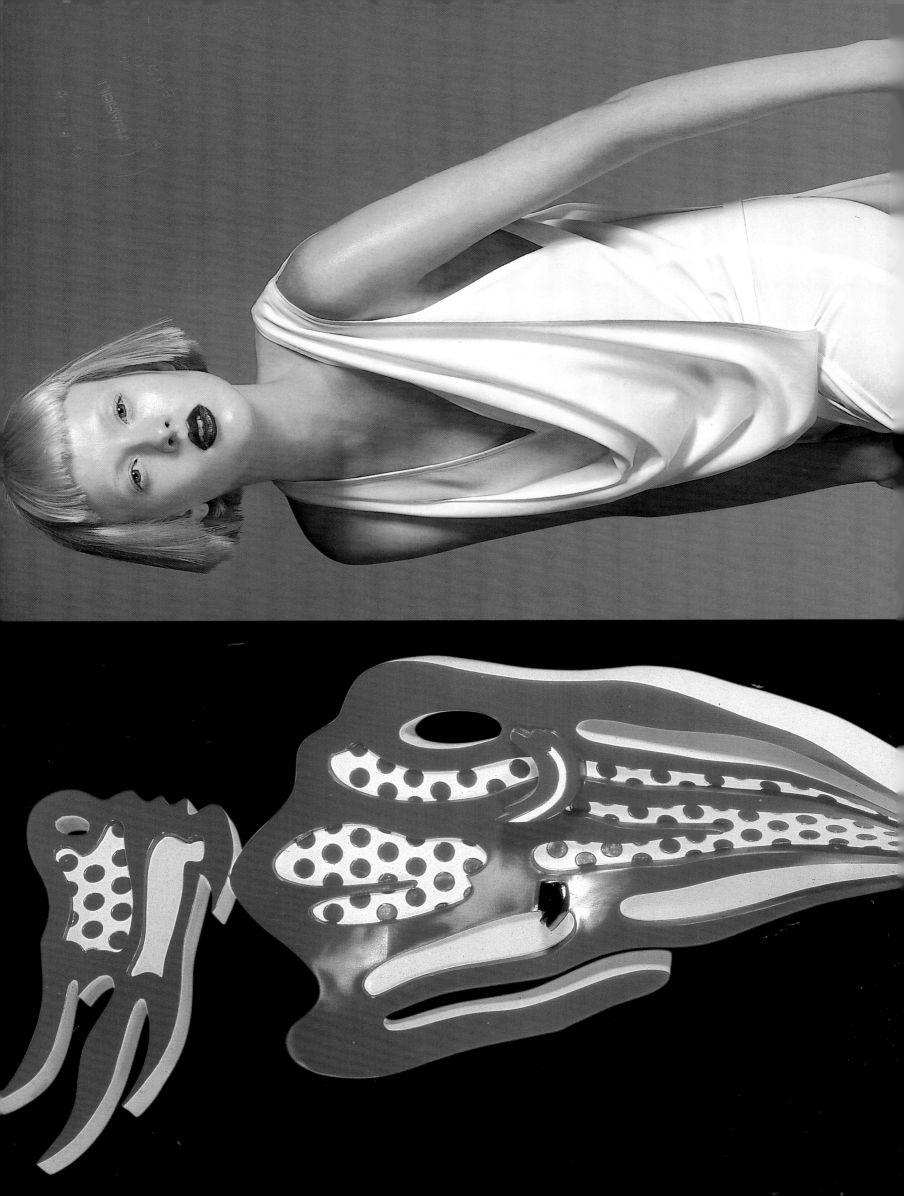

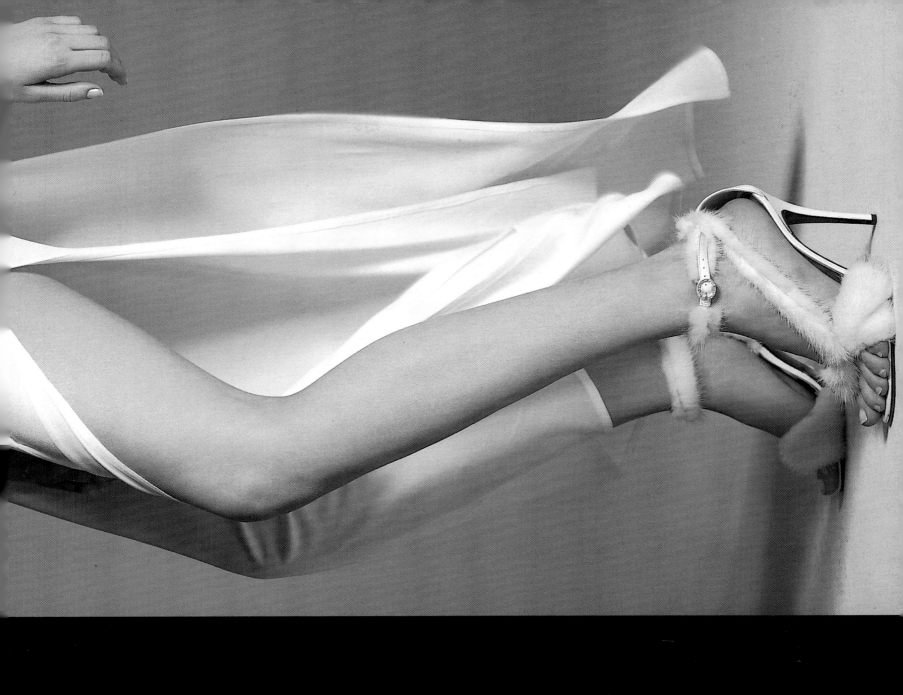
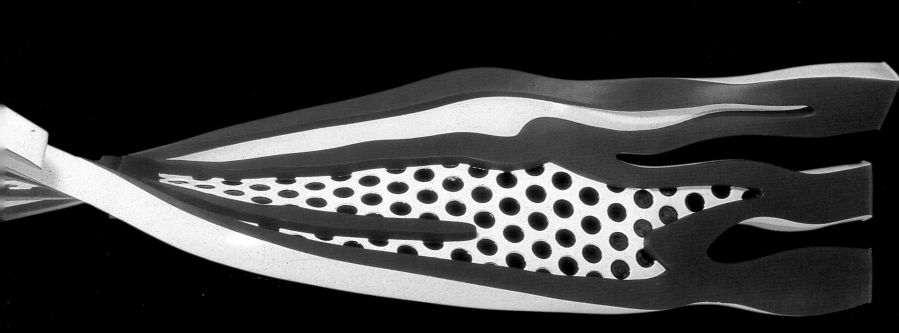

Although I spent time with Gianni, in other ways I know him best from painting his portrait. I actually did it twice. Gianni wasn't the kind of person to embrace art just once. He wasn't the kind of person who would have one work of art by an artist just to say he had one. It went beyond just embracing it. He embraced it like his total embrace of life. He knew art was a way of communing with people through time ... a way of making something real, something that would be there, that goes beyond words. I wanted to paint him because of his voracious need to be touched by art. His need was so unusual. He did not have a voyeuristic relationship ... he wanted to be imbedded in it. From the time he asked me to do his portrait to the moment he was actually standing in the studio and we began to work I experienced his *faith* (in it) that was a big responsibility. I thought "this better look like him when it's done." I didn't want to disappoint him .... And maybe more to the point is that he didn't disappoint me (when I painted him). When you are with someone for a good two hours looking in their eyes and they are standing ten inches away from your face, you see a lot if they have got it to give, and Gianni did. In the curve or the thickness of a lip, the direction of a chronic crease in a brow, resilient posture ... the reflection of water in an eye, the chant-like murmur of unconscious exchange, the daylight changing everything every moment, you can see their strength, their weakness, their vulnerability, all of it ... everything, you don't even know what you're seeing. You're in a trance with them. Something unsaid is happening to both of you. We took a trip together. And Gianni did not just travel with me—or with anybody: he was the captain. In the first portrait he seems to be standing back more, sort of ruling from a distance, his pride dictated the light, he radiated yellow, red, it feels like gold. Looking at it now he seemed older in it; I see his will, his determination. In the second portrait which is essentially blue, and was painted just a few months ago, he was much younger and definitely a *sailor*. He had seen a painting of mine with Prussian blue over Venetian red. He was fixed on this color. In the making of that portrait I found out that blue really is his color. I don't know if it's because he's

Mediterranean or if it's something about the open air which is somehow how I always see him. But the more blue I put in the painting the happier he was and, now that he had the blue he wanted, he said "it's magic when you write words on the paintings, could you put some words on it?" I thought it was done, but I found myself writing "Mi Amigo Gianni." I'm glad I did.... I looked at it and thought he's right, he is my friend. Not just mine... if you look around you'll see that. And he loved his family: so much so that if there was something he loved he wanted them to have one too. He'd seen a steel bed I'd made and asked if I'd make one for him; of course he wanted it to be blue. I made it gold because it was a bed for a King. The bed situation grew. He wanted five beds—for the house in New York—beds for everybody. He wanted beds for each house. The point is that there was no end to his enthusiasm and his generosity. He wanted everyone in his family to share his pleasure. He wanted Antonio to have a portrait, and when I painted him I saw the beauty that Gianni saw in Antonio. He sent Allegra and Daniel and little Antonio, Santo's son, to the studio to be painted. He wanted a portrait of his sister Donatella as a Medusa. His love for Art went beyond attraction. It had to do with Gianni's humanity; he wanted to touch it. And he did. Because he really got it. **Julian Schnabel**

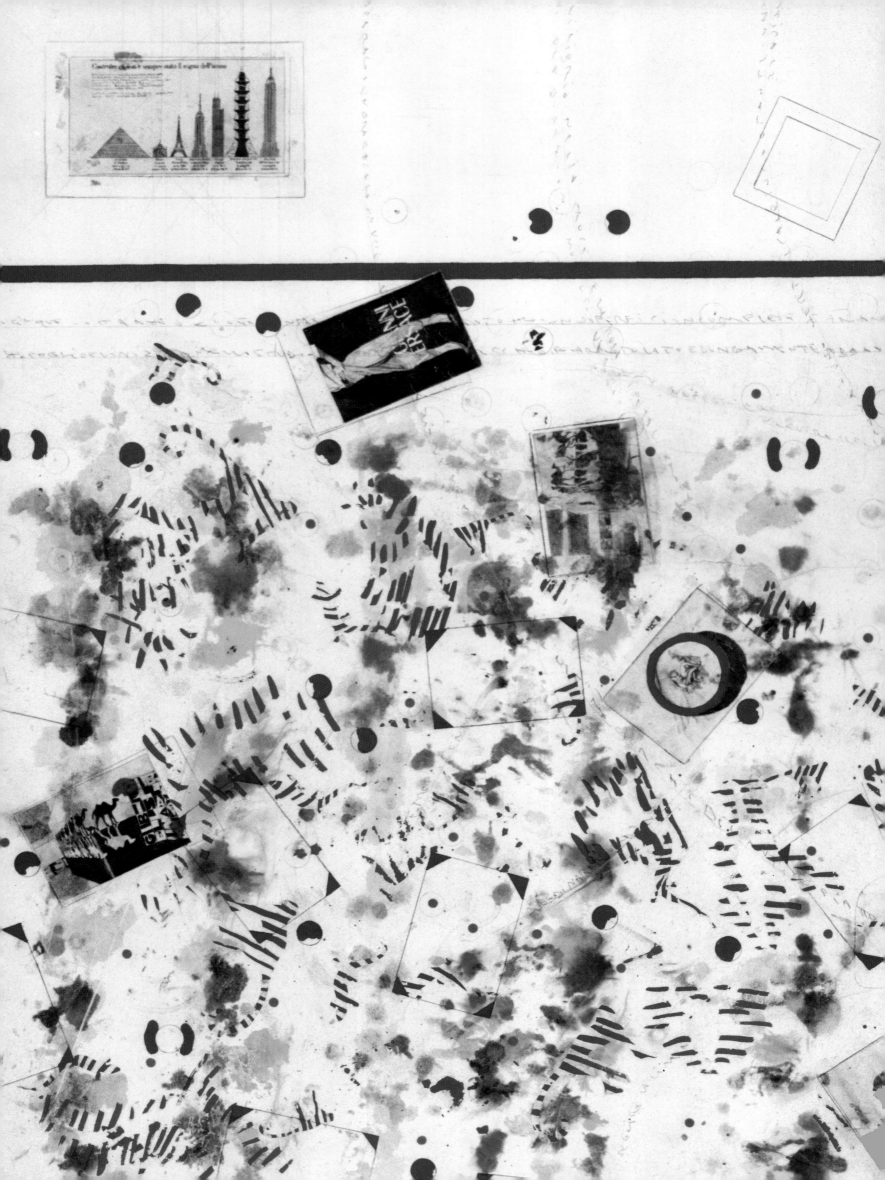

different and
outstanding but also
shy and withdrawn.
They say he often
works outside the
mainstream of his
contemporaries
because, although
always looking into
the future, his
knowledge of the
past makes him
better understand
his own era.

THE WORLD OF G

60

TEATRO ALLA SCALA

ENTE AUTONOMO

STAGIONE D'OPERA E BALLETTO 1983-84
(395ª dalla fondazione del Teatro)

r. N. 20                                                                Turno

MERCOLEDÌ 11 GENNAIO 1984 - ORE 20
PRIMA RAPPRESENTAZIONE

LIEB UND LEID
(Amore e dolore)
Balletto su musica di
GUSTAV MAHLER
(Adagio " dalla Sinfonia n. 10 - Soggetto di ANTONELLO MADAU DIAZ
(Edizione Universal, Wien - Rappr. Ricordi & Co., S.p.A. Milano)

La donna (Eva)    ANGELO MORETTO  Konrad    FRANCESCO SEDENO
DROVANDI  PHILIP BEAMISH    STEFANO BENDINI    UMBERTO BERG
HILLO    MATTEO BUONGIORNO    IVAN CAVALLARI    VITTORIO D'AMA
DI BISCEGLIE    EMILIO GRITTI    GIORGIO MADIA    FRANK PERRA
IANO PESCHINI    RODRIGO RUDAS    ANTONIO RUG IE O    SERGIO S
TAMELLINI    LUCA TONINI    MAURIZIO VANADIA    N DO ZINGONI
Pittore scenografo realizzatore ROBERTO LUCIDI

JOSEPHSLEGENDE
(La leggenda di Giuseppe)
Azione coreografica in un atto
Musica di
RICHARD STRAUSS
rstner, Bad Bramstedt - Rappr. esclusivo per l'Italia: Casa Musicale Sonzogno
Introduzione con strumenti a percussione DAVID SEARC

NA SAVIGNANO Moglie di Putifarre     JOSEPH RUSSI LO  Gius
LO Giacobbe     ANGELO M
ci Una schiava
DRO

A. A. H. P.

عابد عباس حیدری

❈ پروڈیوسر ❈

STATE REFORESTATION AREA PLANTED WITH TREES TO PRODUCE TIMBER BE CAREFUL WITH...

Wildlife Management Area

"I love you," Gianni told me. It was "Darling" over and over, in faxes, in person and on the phone. Of course, this seemed like just another social lubricant, but after a year or so, I began to wonder. I knew he was turned on by the paintings he had commissioned from me, first to fill his living room, and then his dining room on 64th Street. I knew he loved talented people. But he was also supportive in others ways—underwriting an AIDS event I was involved with, and reducing my stress level when I had a bout of cancer. Now I think that if it was not love, it was perhaps the possibility of love. Whatever it was, my collaboration with Gianni was extremely positive. He provoked and energized and I loved painting for him. I loved the delight he took in the art, the music, and the theater that surrounded him and Antonio, and I continue to hear his repeated cry, after a Thai dinner in Soho, "*voglio ballare!*" Frank Moore

Episodes in the

ANTONIO & Eagle

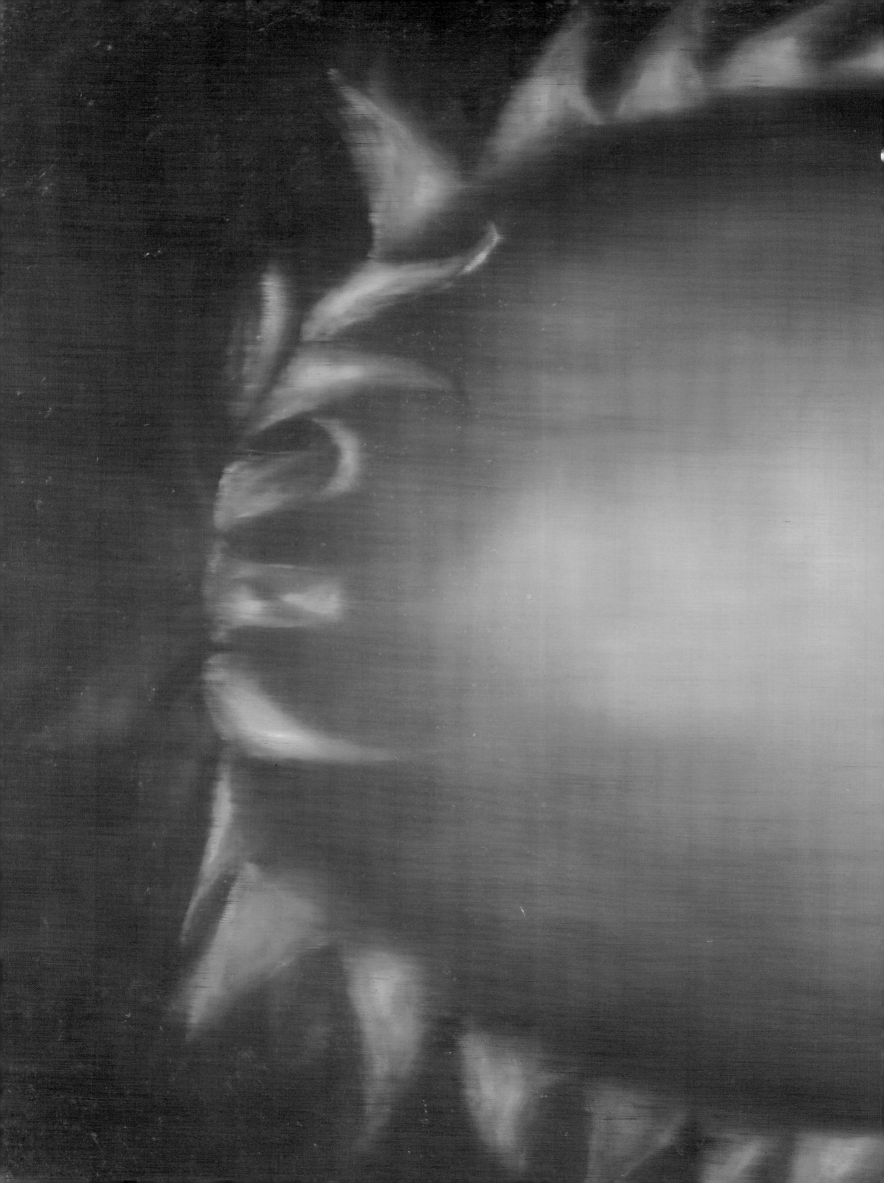

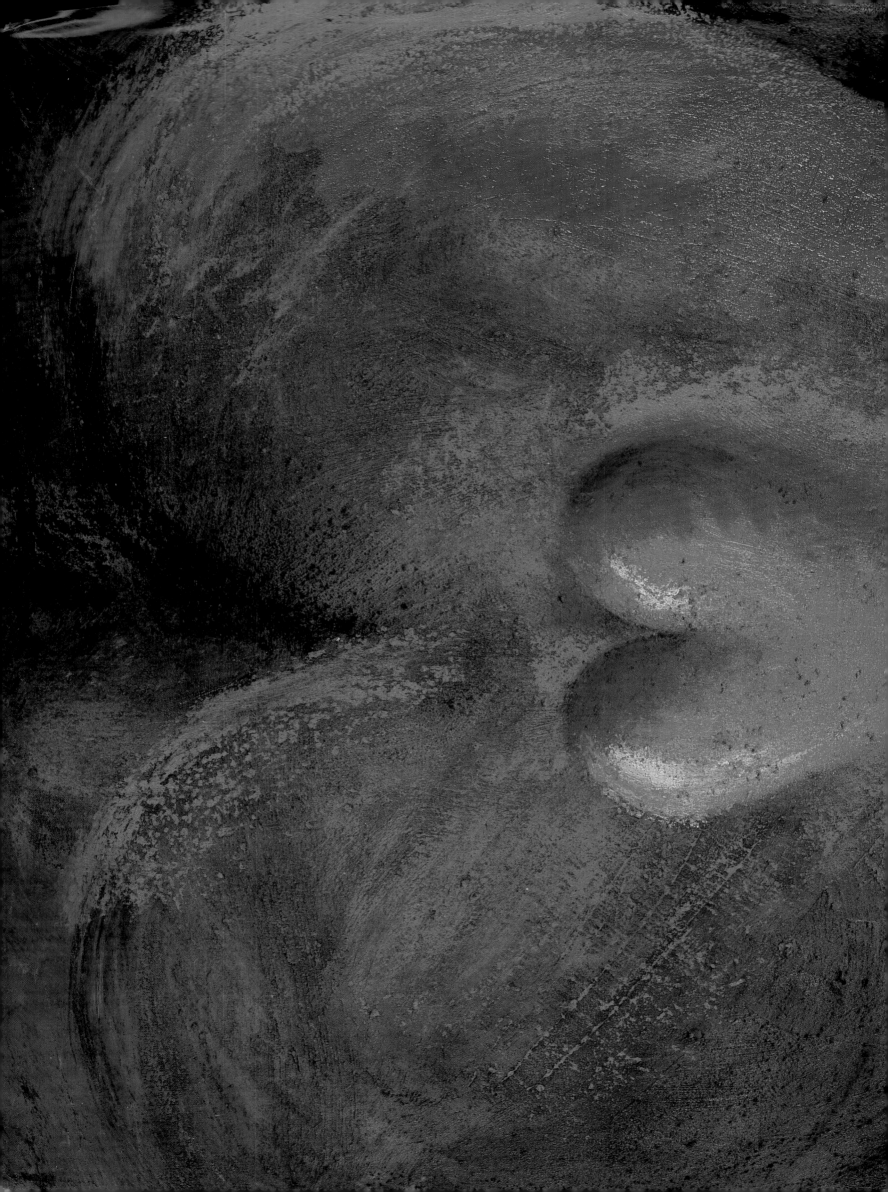

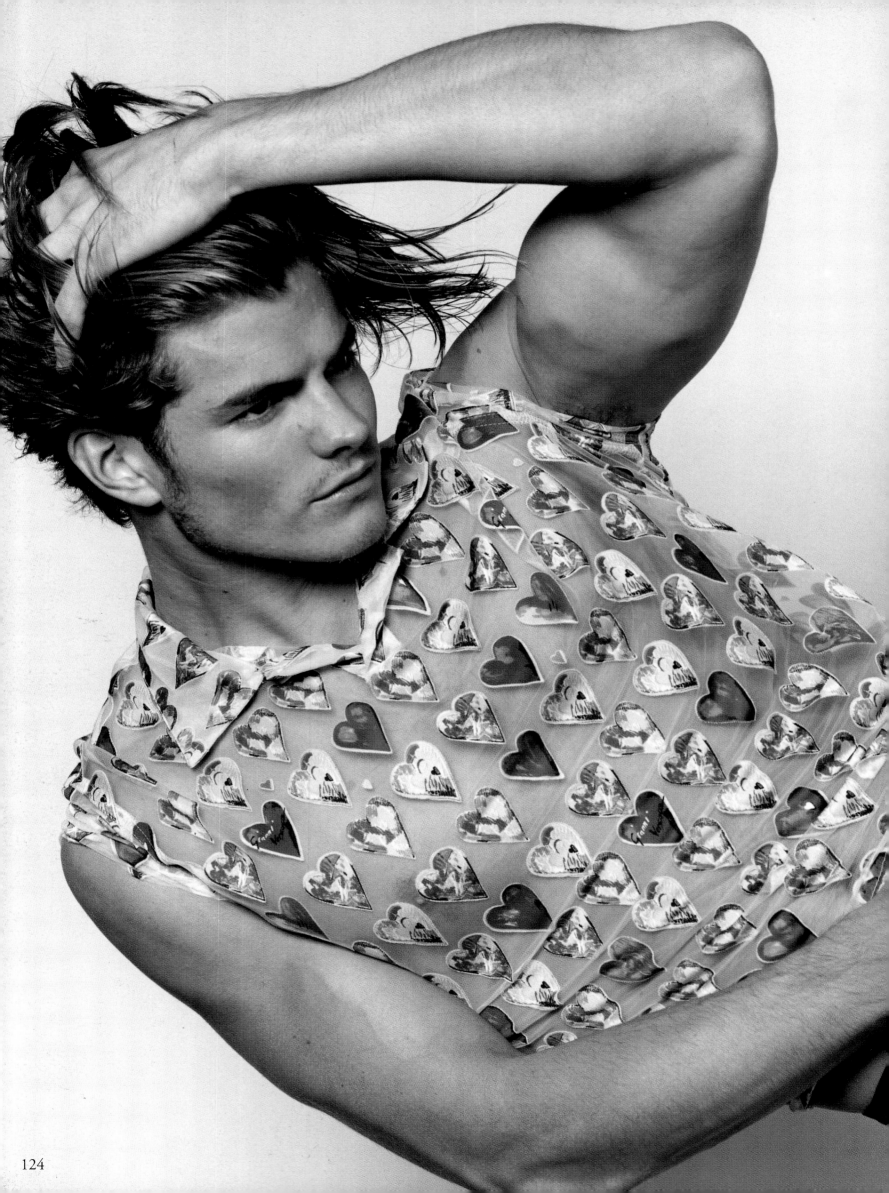

☺ You are one of the people who "goes places in life." ☺

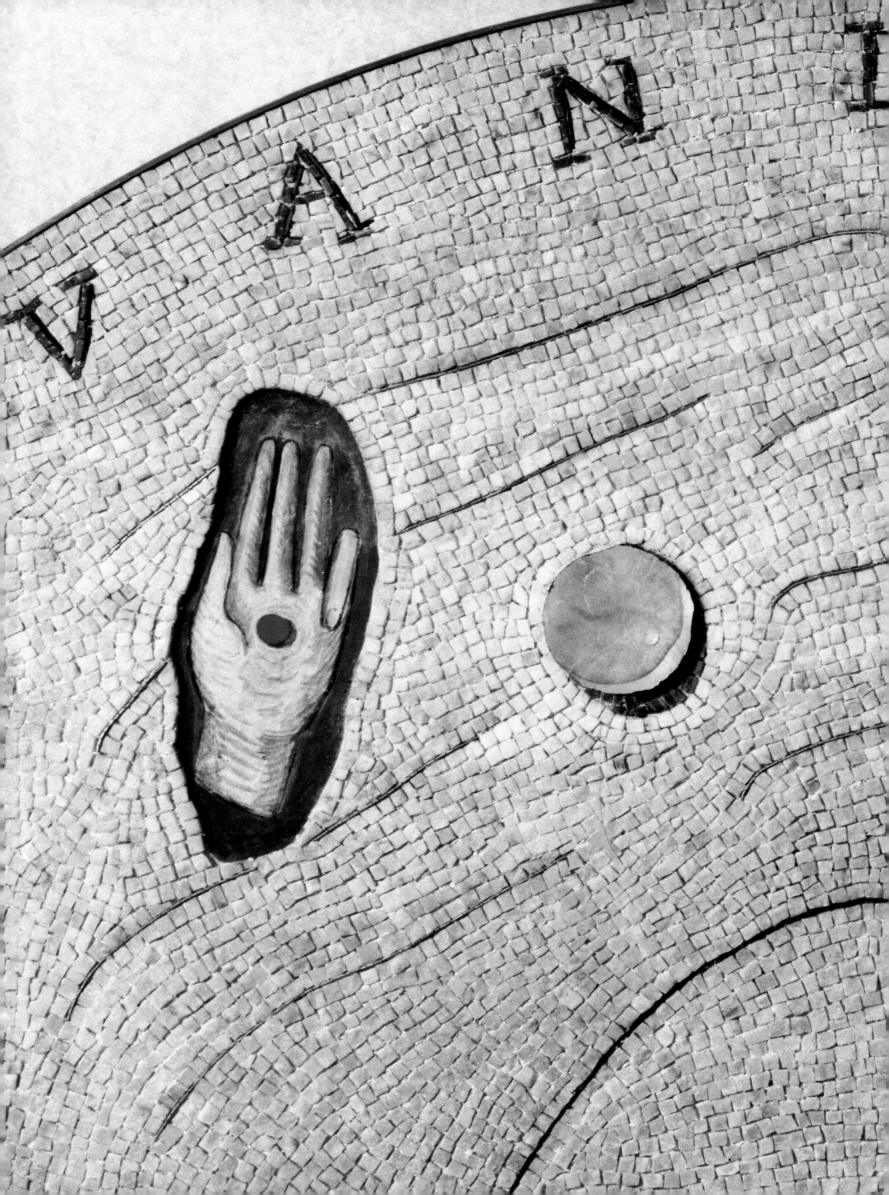

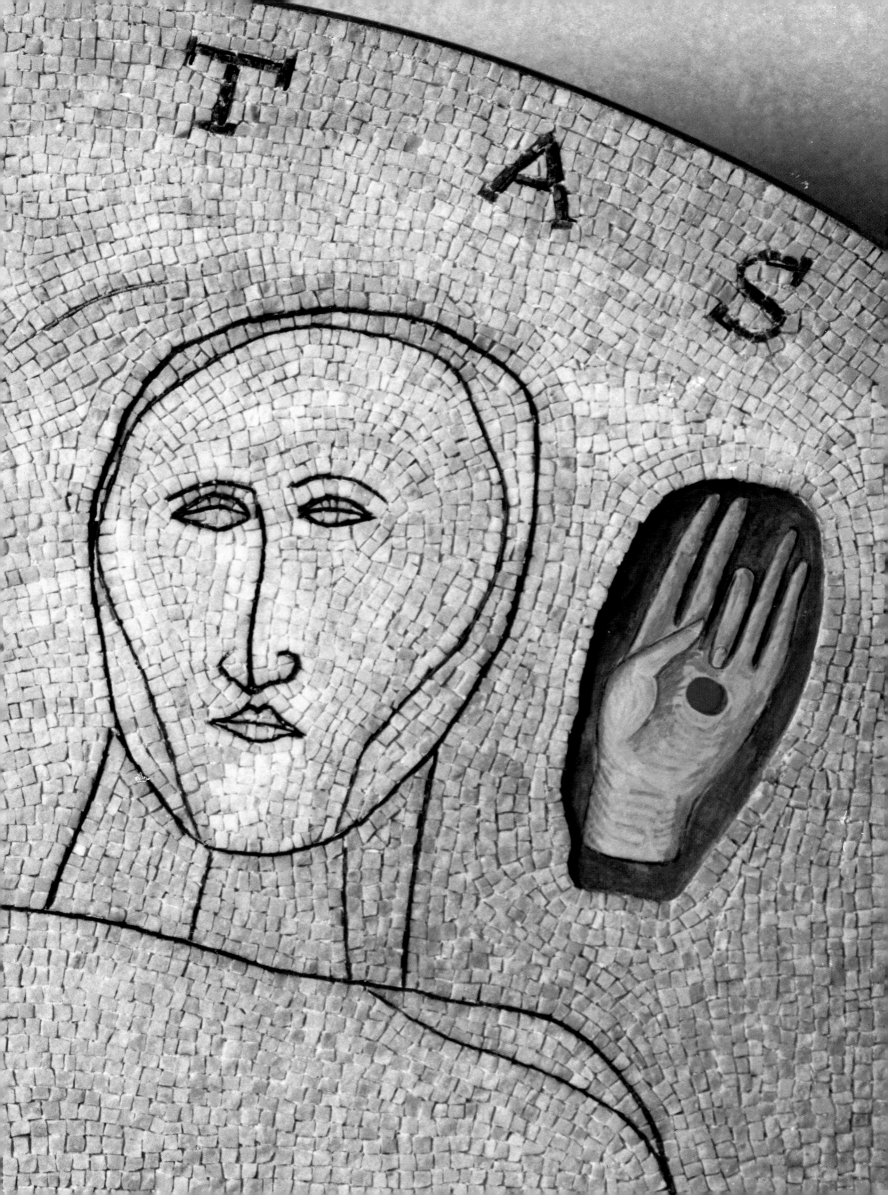

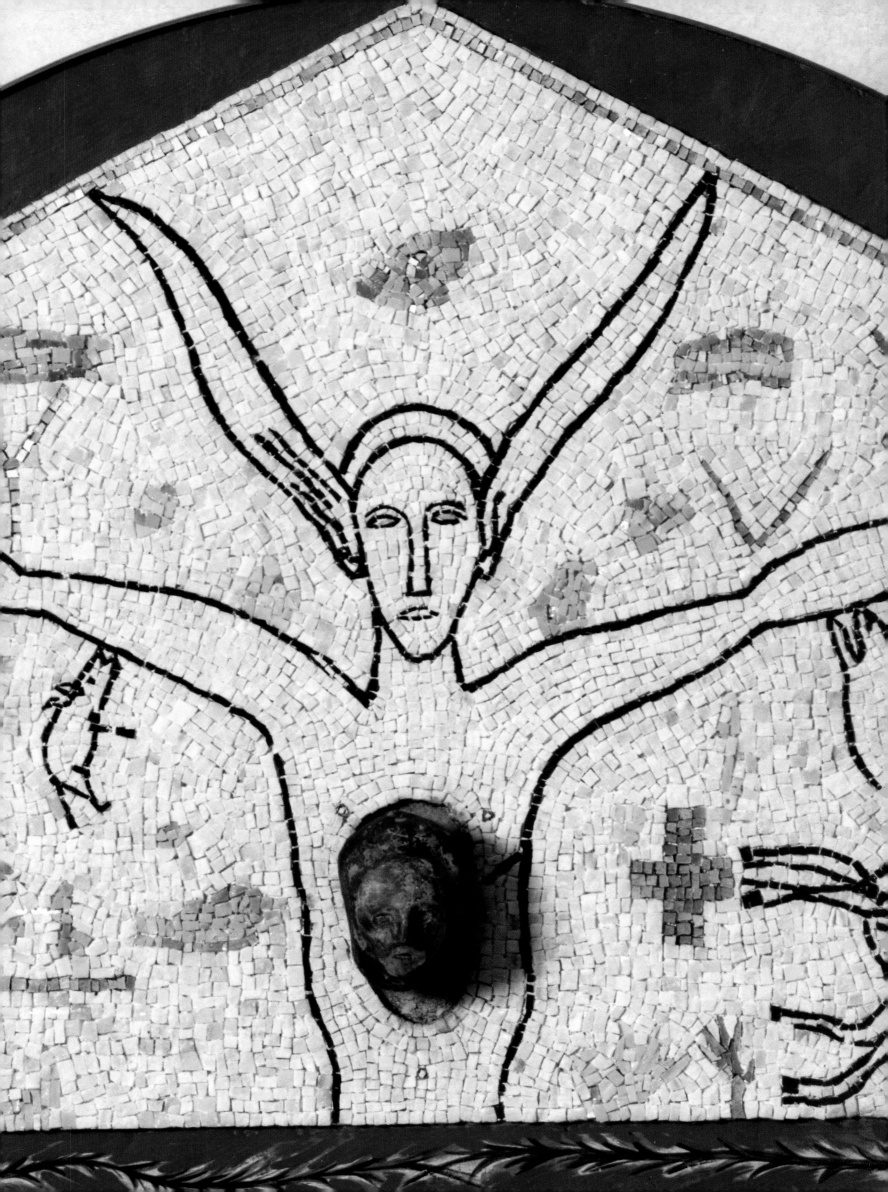

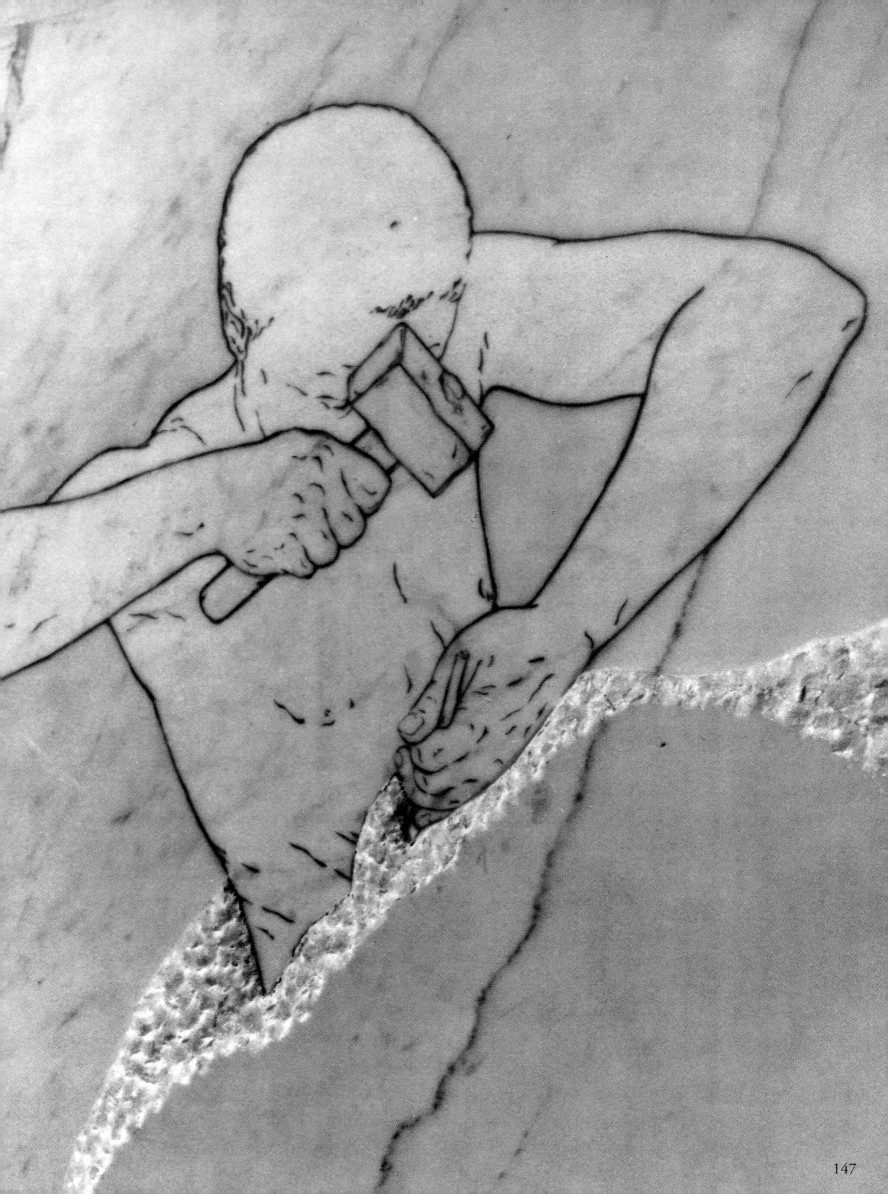

147

Like Pygmalion. Long ago, Ovid recounted the legend of an inhabitant of Cyprus called Pygmalion. After carving a statue of a woman, he was so seduced by its beauty that he fell in love with it, as if it were alive. Obsessed by this passion, the sculptor asked Venus, the goddess of Love, for help. She responded by turning the statue into a living woman. And so the artist and his creation were able to live together. In the present, the story is told of Gianni Versace's passion for classical, modern and contemporary art and of his continual exploration of the concept of beauty through a fascination with living statues and their second skin, clothing. Like Pygmalion, Versace combined his attraction to the body with a quest for the sublime in existence, translated into the form of a dress or a surface and into vital shapes, made of fabrics and colors, techniques and cuts, forms and compositions. Once again Venus intervenes to transform his creations into instruments of living seduction. She dissolves or softens the rigid outlines of his statues or his models to create something that is fluctuating and soft, elegant and sensitive. It is an encounter between tradition and experimentation, between representation and creation, out of which new objects are constructed, transforming our perception of the reality of bodies, so that they are brought to life in another dimension. Like Pygmalion. **Germano Celant**

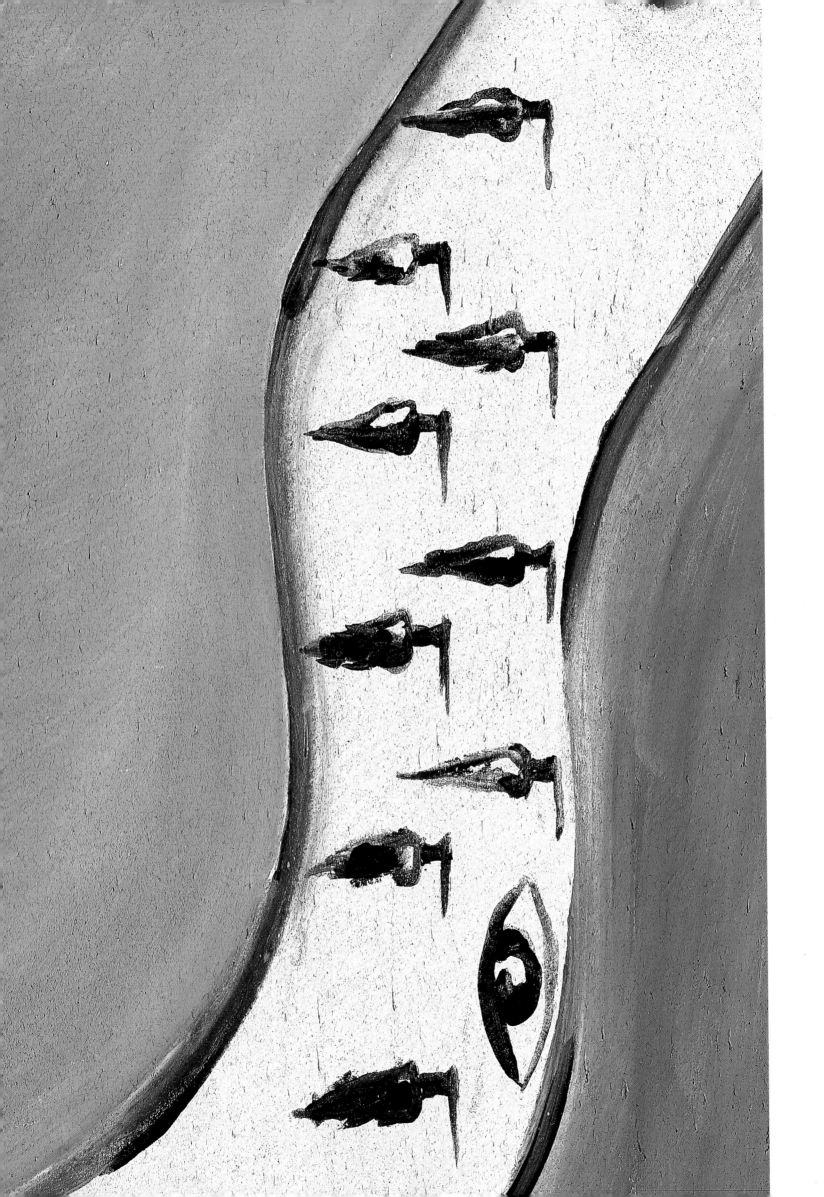

184

Il 3 Maggio 1990 scorre sulla famiglia
di 3 papaveri al sole l'idea di Bellezza:
3 sguardi lunghi, il destino lungo del
...zo occhio rovesciato del quadro - l'idea è la
...nità incosciente dell'opera senza chiedere
chiarimenti -
3 punti bellissimi, naturalmente, mai
3 nel frattempo alla bellezza abbiamo
...nato, senza privilegi, e per te!
L'ispirazione è il cane addomesticato
nell'angola sti cane, magari alla
fine di Aprile -
Se tu fossi quel quadro...tempo lunghi.

G.V. ... maggio 1990

T. PEREZ

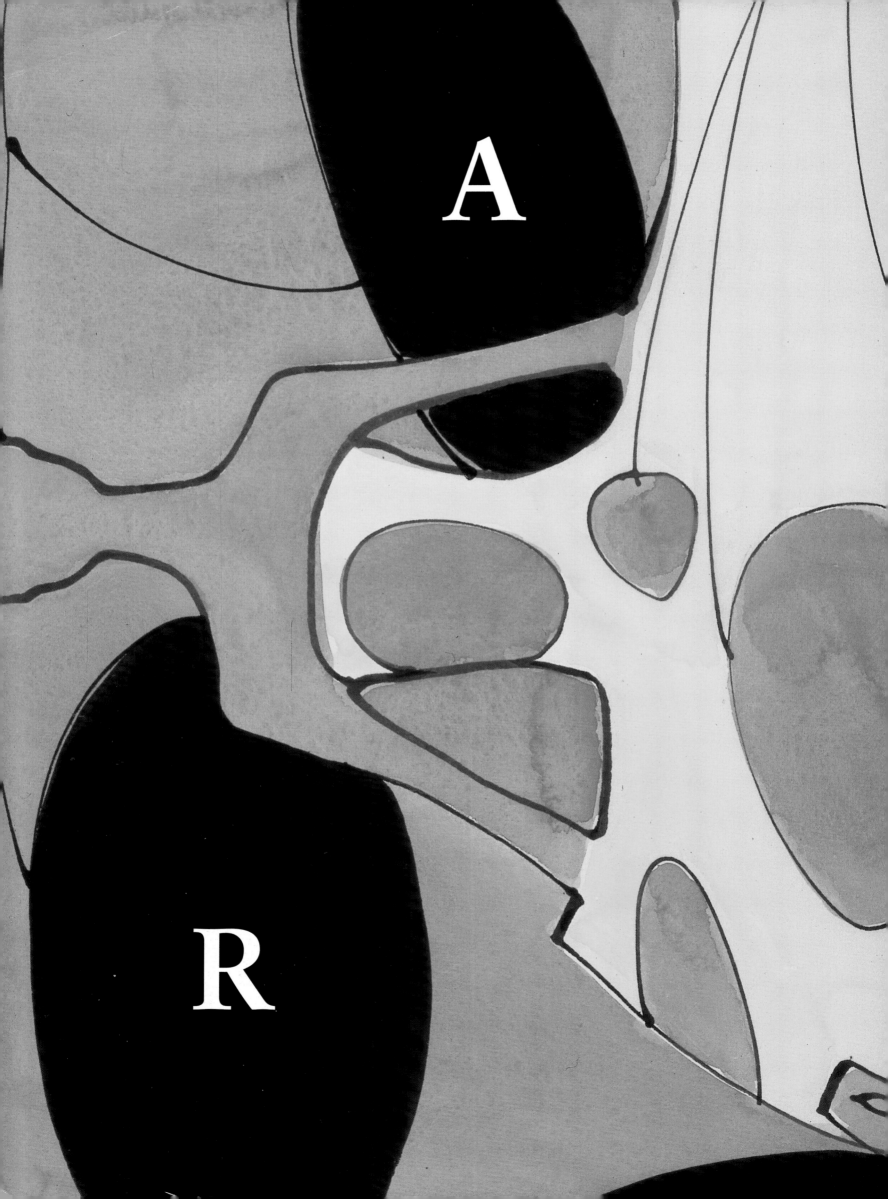

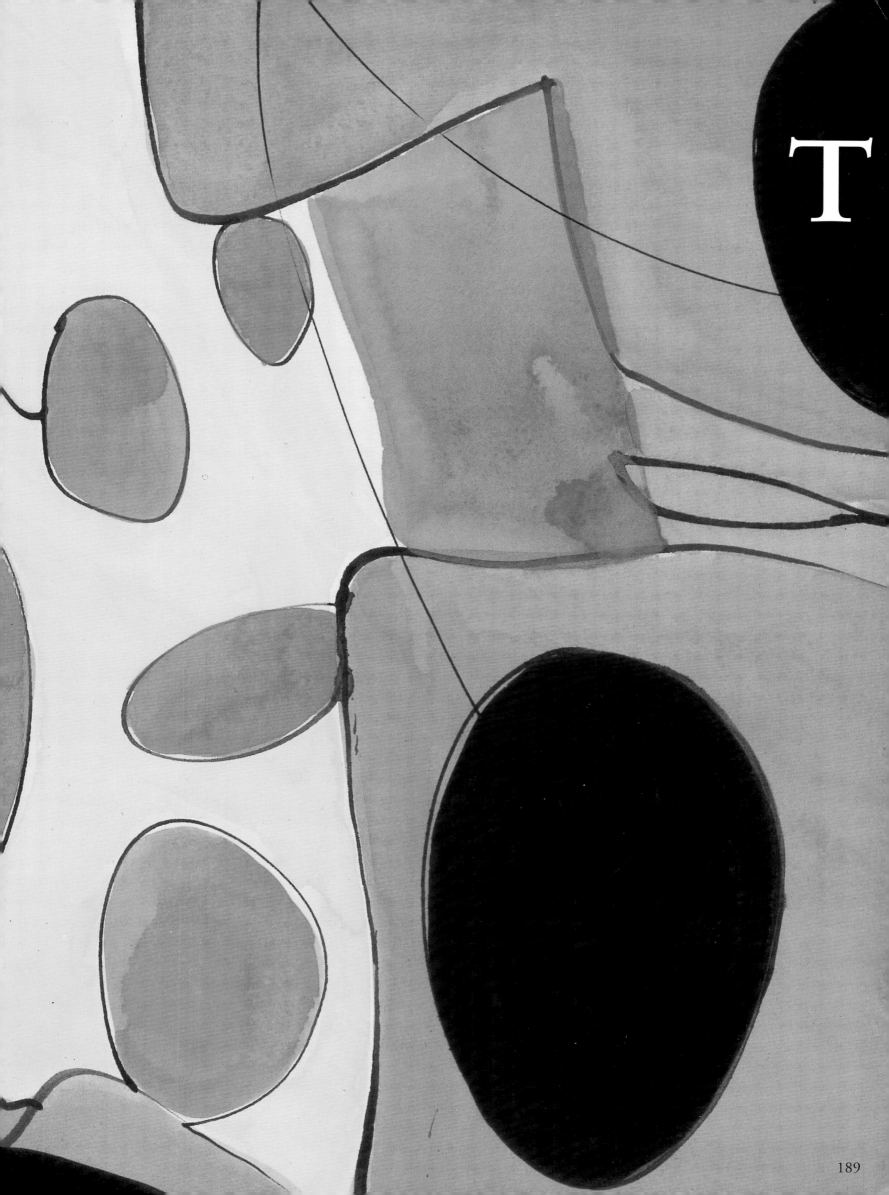

T

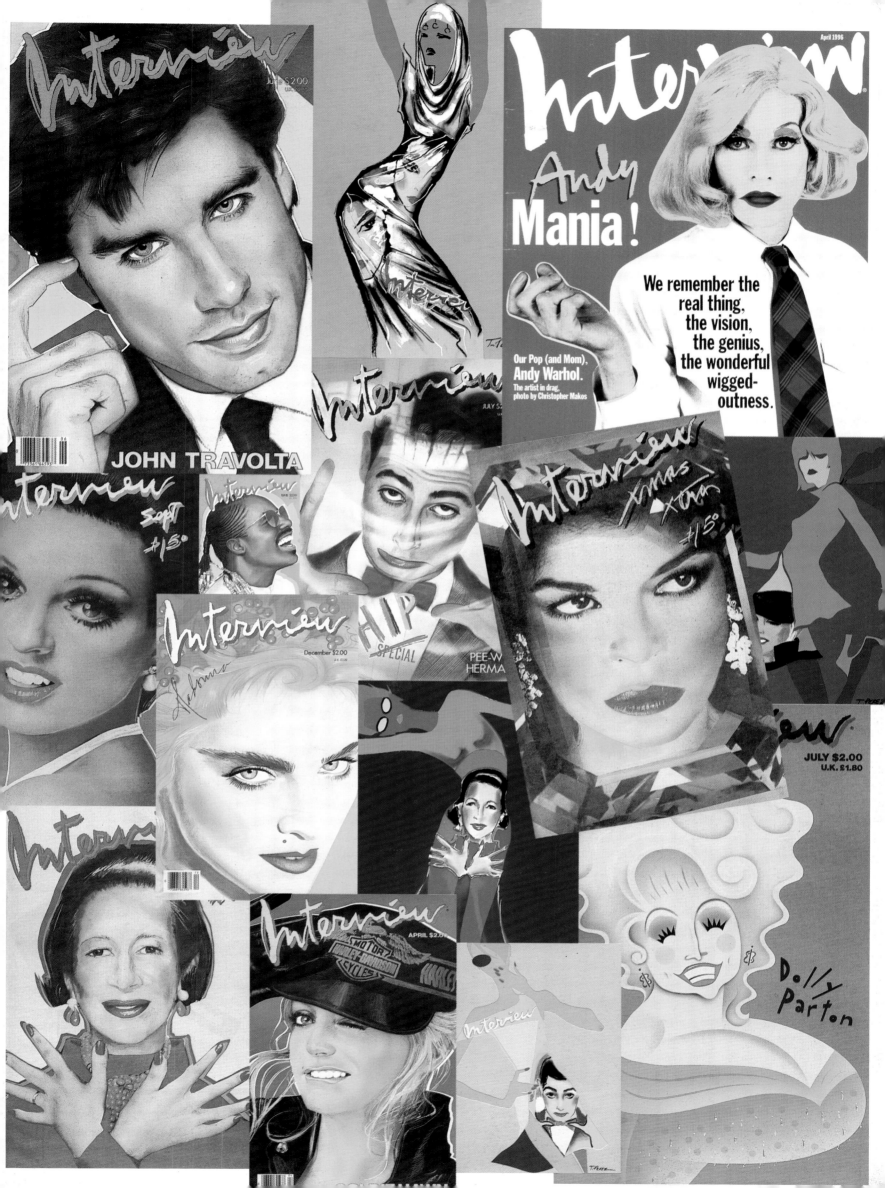

194

Il Vedente m. [signature] 1997

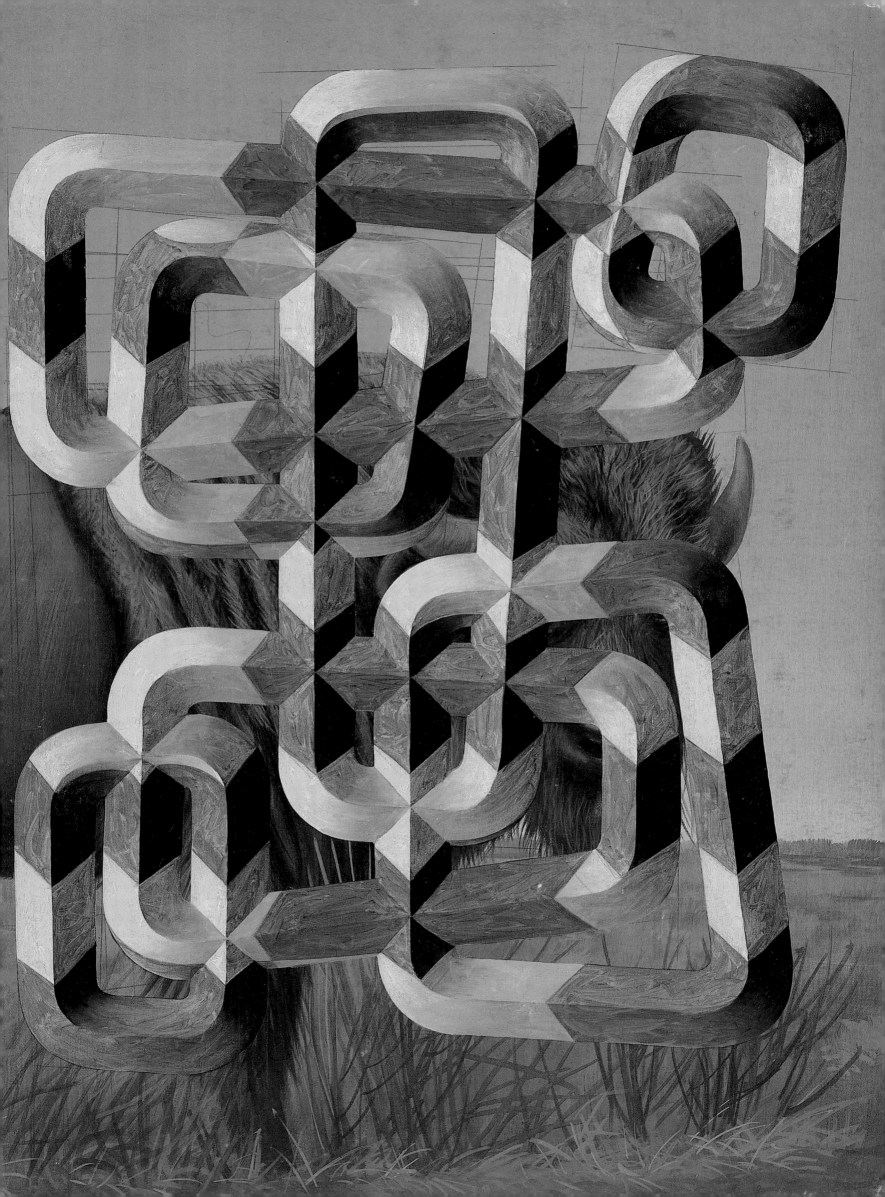

Art direction: GIANNI VERSACE, DONATELLA VERSACE, PAUL BECK

Creative consultant: LUCA STOPPINI

Graphics: LUISA RAPONI, CONSTANCE ASTBURY, ENRICO GENEVOIS

Picture research: TATIANA MATTIONI, FABRIZIA CURZIO, ANNAMARIA STRADELLA

Archives: STEFANIA S. DI GILIO, ANNALISA LUCCHINI, ROBERTO FRANCIERI

Press office: GIANNI VERSACE PRESS OFFICE

General coordination: PATRIZIA CUCCO


Photographs:

RICHARD AVEDON: pp. 8-14-38/39-40-44-84-91-114-128-132-134-140-151-158-166-170/171-184-190-197-200-203-204-208/209-218/219-222/223-244

GIOVANNI GASTEL: pp. 88-122-130

MARIO TESTINO: pp. 98/99-102/103-106-109-110/111

BRUCE WEBER: pp. 15-20-31-33-34-35-54-55-58-60-62-64-67-68-72-75-80-94-112-113-118-121-123-124-127-139-144-146-163-174-176-179-180-194-211-216-227-231-234-239-240


Models:

KAREN ELSON, LINDA EVANGELISTA, KRISTEN MCMENAMY, KATE MOSS, KIRSTEN OWEN, STEPHANIE SEYMOUR, STELLA TENNANT, AMY WESSON


Drawings:

THIERRY PEREZ: pp. 43-45-167-168-173-174-187-191-198-213-214-225-233-236


The published photographic material comes from the archives of Gianni Versace Spa, with the exception of the following photographs:

MICHEL COMTE: Philip Taaffe working in his studio, *l'Uomo Vogue*, January 1996, pp. 28/29

MATS GUSTAFSON: *A+C Anthology*, Italian *Vogue*, March 1997, pp. 188/189; *Vogue* Italia, October 1984, pp. 184-185;

STEVEN MEISEL: *A+C Anthology*, Italian *Vogue*, January 1997, pp. 22/23-24/25-26/27

Gianni Versace and Antonio D'Amico: Julian Schnabel working in his studio, pp. 46-53


Cover: Portrait of Gianni Versace by Andy Warhol.

Back cover: Photo by Bruce Weber for the 1997 Spring/Summer men's collection.

Front endpaper: *Amphitrites*, 1925, cape by Paul Poiret; Sketch for *Souvenir de Léningrad*, 1987, by Bruno Gianesi

Back endpaper: Sketch of a dress, Tullio Crali, 1932; *Chevaux marins et coquillages*, 1925, cape by Paul Poiret; *Woman in Evening Dress*, 1925, Giacomo Balla (Biagiotti-Cigna collection); Sketch for *La mort subite*, 1991, by Bruno Gianesi

© 1997 by Leonardo Arte srl, Milan

Elemond Editori Associati

All rights reserved under international copyright conventions. No part of this book may be reproduced

or utilized in any form or by any means, electronic or mechanical, including photocopying, recording,

or by any information storage and retrieval system, without permission in writing from the publisher.

Inquiries should be addressed to Abbeville Press, 22 Cortlandt Street, New York, N.Y. 10007.

Printed and bound in Italy.

First U.S. edition


10 9 8 7 6 5 4 3 2 1


ISBN 0-7892-0436-3

Art:

DONALD BAECHLER: Artwork (including family photograph of Gianni Versace as a child) created especially for *The Art of Being You*, from Gianni Versace, a special supplement for *Interview* magazine's October 1996 issue, p. 126

ROSS BLECKNER: *The Hope for News*, 1996, pp. 96/97; *Calling Each Other by Name*, 1996, pp. 116/117

ALIGHIERO BOETTI: *Senza titolo*, 1990, pp. 56/57; *Senza titolo*, p. 61; *Pulcinella*, 1992, p. 65

ENZO CUCCHI: *Più vicino alla luce VI*, 1996, pp. 152/153; *Più vicino alla luce VII*, 1996, pp. 154/155 (detail), 156/157

FRANCESCO CLEMENTE: Medusa watercolors especially created for *The Art of Being You*, from Gianni Versace, a special supplement for *Interview* magazine's October 1996 issue, pp. 129-131-135

JIM DINE: *Portrait of Antonio*, 1996, p. 85; *Gianni's Heart*, 1996, pp. 118/119; *Gianni's Portrait*, 1996, p. 125; *Medusa*, 1996, p. 133

ROY LICHTENSTEIN: *Brushstroke Nude*, 1993, pp. 38/39; *Blue Nude*, 1995, p. 41; *Untitled*, 1997, p. 42

JASPER JOHNS: *Between the Clock and the Bed* (detail), 1981, collection of the artist, p. 172

WASSILY KANDINSKY: *Black Form*, 1923, collection Mr. and Mrs. Joseph Lauder, p. 164

ELLSWORTH KELLY: *Black Ripe*, 1955, collection of Harry W. and Mary Margaret Anderson, p. 183

HENRI MATISSE: Back cover of *Verve* magazine, n. 1, December 1937, p. 186

SEBASTIAN MATTA: *Senza titolo 2*, 1992, p. 115; *Senza titolo 1*, 1992, p. 159

FRANK MOORE: *Cow*, 1996, pp. 70/71; *Stretch*, 1996, p. 73; *Wildlike Management Area*, 1990, p. 74; *Frank Moore's Studio*, 1995, pp. 89-92/93-95; *Untitled*, 1995, photographs by Todd Eberle, pp. 86/87-90

MIMMO PALADINO: *Vanitas II*, 1990, pp. 136/137; *Vanitas I*, 1990, p. 141; *Untitled*, 1992, pp. 142/143; *Letter to Versace*, 1990, p. 185; *Il vedente*, 1997, p. 196; *La sera dei miracoli*, 1996, p. 199; *La sera dei miracoli: testa fiorita*, 1996, p. 201; *La sera dei miracoli: camera rumorosa dei passi teatrali lungo il perimetro respiro e canto*, 1995, p. 202; *La sera dei miracoli: luglio, agosto, il vulcano*, 1995, p. 205; *Medusa*, 1997, pp. 206/207; *Poeta da camera*, 1992, p. 212; *Spiriti che abitate l'universo delle stanze*, 1992, p. 215

PABLO PICASSO: *Nus sur la plage*, pp. 220/221; *Paloma*, 1954, p. 224; *Fillette au bateau*, 1938, p. 226; *Enfant à la balle—Claude*, 1948, p. 228; *Paloma dans sa petite chaise*, 1950, p. 229; *Deux bustes de profil*, 1972, p. 230; *Maternité à l'orange*, 1951, p. 232; *Femme assise sur une chaise*, 1938, p. 237

MICHELANGELO PISTOLETTO: *Ritratto di Gianni Versace*, p. 162

MARK ROTHKO: *Untitled*, 1969, p. 169

MIMMO ROTELLA: *Collage*, 1988, p. 59; *Collage*, 1986, p. 63; *Senza titolo*, p. 66; *Senza titolo*, 1986, p. 69; *Collage*, p. 81; *Collage*, 1988, p. 107; *Medusa*, 1997, p. 108

KRIS RUHS: *Medusa*, 1997, p. 32

DAVID SALLE: *Ship in bottle*, 1996, pp. 82/83; *Winter court*, 1996, pp. 104/105

MARIO SCHIFANO: *Casa Versace*, 1990, pp. 160/161-192/193; *Senza titolo*, 1994, pp. 175-177; *Esterno*, 1990, p. 178; *Nottetempo*, 1990, p. 181; *Sovraesposto*, 1990, p. 195

JULIAN SCHNABEL: *Portrait of Gianni*, 1995, p. 47; *Gianni Versace*, 1996, p. 50; *Portrait of Allegra and Daniel*, 1996, p. 51; *Portrait of Antonio*, 1995, p. 52

PETER SCHUYFF: *Five American Paintings*, 1997, pp. 210-217-238-241; Photograph for Gianni Versace by Bruce Weber. Courtesy of Gianni Versace archives. Artwork created by Peter Schuyff especially for *The Art of Being You*, from Gianni Versace, a special supplement for *Interview* magazine's October 1996 issue, pp. 246-247; Photograph for Gianni Versace by Richard Avedon. Courtesy of Gianni Versace archives. Artwork created by Peter Schuyff especially for Gianni Versace, pp. 242/243-245-248

PHILIP TAAFFE: *Untitled*, 1995/96, p. 21; *Nocturne*, 1995/96, pp. 22/23; *Untitled*, 1995, p. 30; *Figure with Excavated Crescents*, 1995/96, pp. 36/37; *Saint John's Gate*, 1993, pp. 78/79

ANTONIO TROTTA: *Bas-relief*, pp. 138-145-147-150

ANDY WARHOL: *Alert CE*, 1984/85, pp. 6/7; *GE Man in Green Stripe*, 1984/85, p. 9; *Amoco*, 1984, pp. 10/11; *In the Chiner*, 1982, pp. 12/13; *Interview* magazine covers. Courtesy of *Interview* magazine, pp. 167-191

Royalties from the sale of this book will be donated to the Italian Association for Cancer Research (A.I.R.C.)

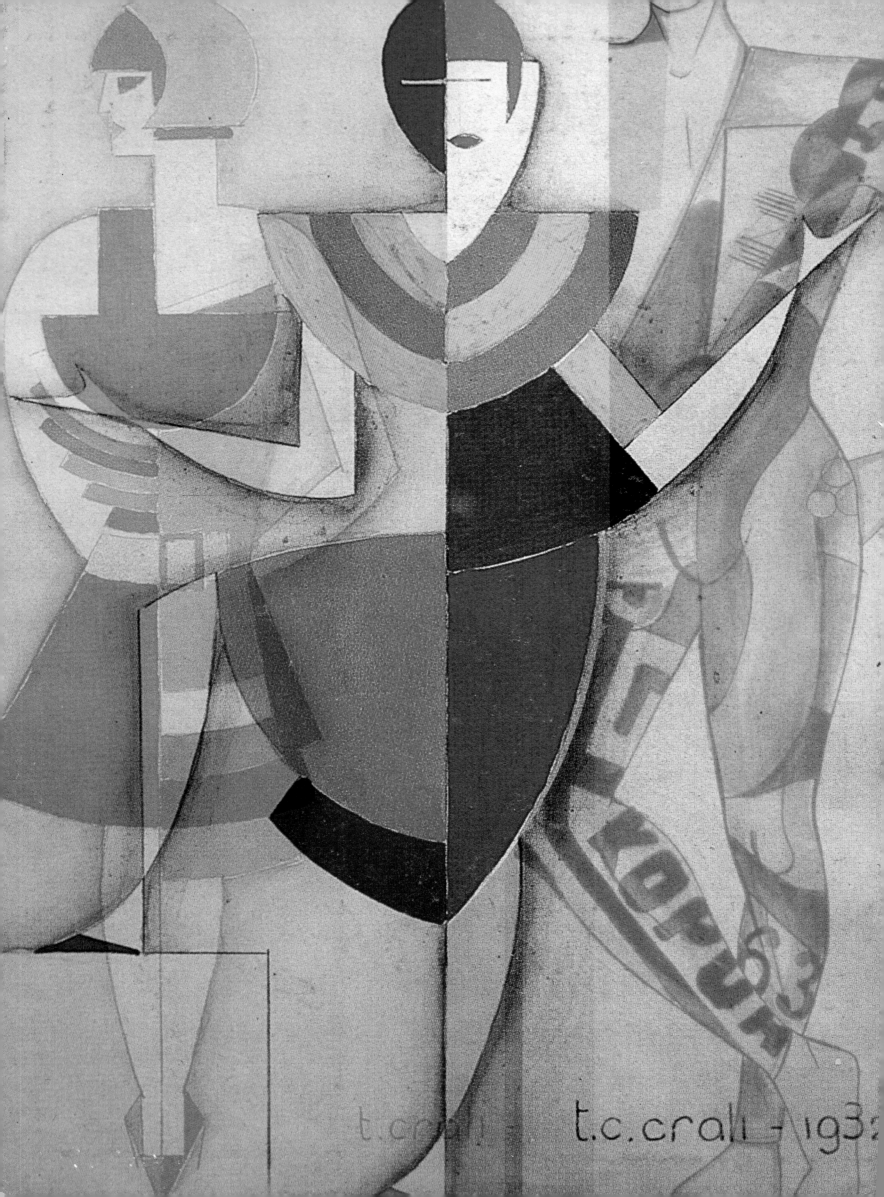